Culinary Arts Institute®

CROCKERY COOKING

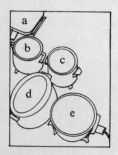

Featured in cover photo:
a. **Rosé Baked Apples, 94**
b. **Split Pea Soup, 24**
c. **Multi-Vegetable Beef Stew, 32**
d. **Roast Stuffed Turkey, 69**
e. **Super Turban Cake, 85**

CROCKERY

CROCKERY COOKING

The Culinary Arts Institute Staff:

Helen Geist: Director

Sherrill Corley and Barbara MacDonald: Editors

Ethel La Roche: Editorial Assistant • Ivanka Simatic: Recipe Tester

Edward Finnegan: Executive Editor • Malinda Miller: Copy Editor

Charles Bozett: Art Director • John Mahalek: Art Assembly

Book designed and coordinated by Charles Bozett and Laurel DiGangi

Illustrations by Gwen Connelly

COOKING

Adventures in Cooking SERIES

Culinary Arts Institute®

1975 North Hawthorne, Melrose Park, Illinois 60160

FOREWORD

In this jet age, why all the excitement about the slow-cooking pot? While the rest of the world rushes on, it takes its own sweet time, producing dishes reminiscent of a more leisurely past.

To find out, Culinary Arts Institute has spent several months putting crocks to the test. Twenty models simmered away in our Test Kitchen, and members of our staff tested at home to see how well they suit the life of the working woman.

The crock's main advantage, we feel, is that it turns out dishes with old-fashioned goodness while adjusting cooking time to suit the cook. Once the food is in the pot and the control turned to Low, you can leave it to its own devices. And you needn't hurry back; dinner will be ready and waiting when you want it.

Just as the watched pot never boils, the unwatched slow cooker never burns. The heat on Low is steady, and the environment is moist because the steam can't escape. Under these conditions, an extension of an hour or so won't harm the food.

Moist heat offers an important fringe benefit—economy. In combination with expanded cooking times, it will tenderize the very cuts of meat that cost the least. It may not be the pot of gold waiting at the end of your rainbow, but it could mean a little left over in the food budget.

During hot weather the crock lets you cook without heating up the kitchen. Stews, soups, pot roasts, quick breads, and cakes—usually reserved for wintry weather—become year-round possibilities.

The slow cooker is a handy hostess tool; it doubles as a keep-warm serving dish. At holiday time a pot of wassail or glögg can simmer away on the buffet without taking up precious space on the range top.

Whether or not it is the all-purpose cooker that some claim is a matter of personal opinion. Some of our testers were enthusiastic about the baked goods from the crock; others thought they'd use it exclusively for soups, stews, and stocks. Few thought they'd take the time to prepare stew ingredients before leaving for work.

We believe that the slow cooker may have gained an unjustified reputation for being a work saver. While it is true that it lets you adjust cooking schedules to your convenience, the total amount of work is' exactly the same when slow cooking or cooking in the standard way. The kinds of recipes that the slow cooker does best are not quick tricks. They are the combination dishes, stews, and medleys that require tasks such as peeling, cutting, and measuring before cooking. With the slow cooker, you can do this preparation when you have the time, and refrigerate the food until cooking time, but your time invested is the same, either way.

But what will matter to you is your own opinion. Base it on experience, not guesswork, by sampling recipes from all the categories. As you get to know your cooker, you'll discover the many ways crock cooking can enhance your own personal cooking style.

CONTENTS

KNOW YOUR COOKER

Confused about crocks? No wonder. There are over a baker's (or slow cooker's) dozen, all vying for your favor. Sorting through their many features can lead a shopper to feel that too many cookers can spoil—if not the broth—his power of decision.

What you want is a cooker that offers the most convenience for the price you want to pay. To help you make a choice, here is a rundown of features offered by the slow-cooking pot.

FEATURES OF THE SLOW COOKER

1. It's an electric appliance. It's heated either by coils around the sides or at the base. At least one has a separate pot that lifts off a base somewhat like a hot plate.

The electricity supplies either continuous heat or is controlled by a thermostat. Continuous-heat pots are those that have High, Low, and Off settings. The thermostatically controlled cooker may allow for settings high enough for such jobs as deep-fat frying.

If you want a cooker that will do more than slow-cook, you may prefer the one with the thermostatic switch. The dial is calibrated to show settings up to 500°F. However, the simple High and Low settings can accomplish what the slow cooker does best. That is the lengthy, no-peek variety of cooking that frees the cook for other things when the crock is turned to Low. The Low setting on continuous-heat cookers maintains a temperature of around 180° to 200°F.

The High setting, which keeps the food at a temperature around 300°F, is a convenience feature. It cooks in half the time of the Low setting and helps when you need to speed things up. But it doesn't offer the same "go away and forget it" kind of cooking. Foods with a high sugar content, such as carrots, can get overly brown at this temperature if left too long.

2. Being electric, the slow cooker has a cord. And this becomes a feature, as some pots have detachable cords, while others have permanent ones. If you plan to use your cooker as a serving piece at the table, the permanent cord may be awkward.

3. The slow cooker is usually shaped like a saucepot with either a round or oval opening. The oval pot is a little more adaptable as it can hold such items as whole birds and ham slices that don't conform to the round shape. Capacity ranges from 2½ to 8 quarts.

4. The cooker has a tight-fitting lid which captures the steam that tenderizes those economical cuts of meat. Some lids have a higher dome than others. Height can be an advantage if you use a makeshift cooker insert, such as a coffee can, as some recipes suggest.

5. The "crock" is usually of ceramic stoneware, but some models have liners of glass or metal. Stoneware and glass hold heat better than metal and stand up under normal wear, but they are breakable. The metal ones can withstand greater changes in temperature.

Some crocks are removable from the metal

casings that hold the heating element. These are easier to wash (after cooling to room temperature) and can be used as a separate serving piece.

6. There may be a signal light. It helps, as it prevents leaving a pot turned on inadvertently. Models with thermostatic controls show a light only when the power is on, not when it cycles off. It switches on again when the temperature in the pot drops below the desired level.

USE AND CARE

Packed along with each new slow cooker is a booklet from the manufacturer. The few minutes it takes to read it through may determine how well you'll like your new appliance.

The booklet will tell you what features make your crock unique, and what techniques to use when cooking with it. Most of the instructions are easy; it's changing old habits that's hard. But once you've discovered the flexibility a slow cooker can bring to cooking, you should have plenty of incentive to adjust.

BEFORE YOU COOK

The manufacturer will tell you to wash the crock before using it. If you have a one-piece model, with crock and heating unit combined, you should wash the inside of the pot only.

But if the crock is removable, it can go right into the dishpan. The metal casing should be wiped clean with a damp cloth so that the electric fittings are kept dry.

Cookers with metal pots can be conditioned by rubbing the cooking surface lightly with cooking oil or shortening.

PLAY IT SAFE

The beauty of crock cooking, they say, is that you can "set it and forget it." And it does offer the unique advantage that food will never burn on the Low setting. It will overcook if left too long, but it can be left for a very long time—eighteen hours or more—without harm. This is because steam can't escape; the moisture is captured inside.

But there are precautions you should take to prevent other mishaps with your cooker.

1. Situate the cooker on a moisture-free, level surface so there is no danger of tipping.

2. Keep the pot out of reach of children and pets. You can go away for extended periods, but if you're leaving it, and the children, with a sitter, caution her as you would about food left cooking on the range.

3. If your cooker has a detachable cord, plug it into the appliance with the dial set at Off before plugging it into the outlet. After cooking, set the switch back to Off before unplugging from the outlet. If the heating element is removable, let the base cool before disconnecting it.

4. Place the pot so that the electric cord won't trip anyone. In the kitchen, set the pot at the back of the counter where it won't interfere with your working space. In the dining room, put it on the buffet or some table near an electric outlet, away from paths of traffic. A hot mat under the cooker will protect the surface of the table.

5. Removable crockery pots are made to give long service when kindly treated. But like any ceramic, they are breakable. They shouldn't be used directly on the range top, in the oven, or outdoors. They shouldn't be used to store food in the refrigerator, then transferred directly to the heating element, as sudden temperature changes can crack them. For the same reason, don't put cold water or frozen foods into the ceramic pot when it's hot. And let the crock cool before putting it into the dishwater.

6. Keep the cooker unplugged when not in use. The dial could accidentally be turned on, running up the electric bill and possibly causing a burn.

7. Protect hands with potholders when handling the heated crock. Removing cooker inserts or coffee cans from a hot pot can be a little tricky. In our Test Kitchen, a wooden spatula was used to slip down one side of the insert and pry it up, while the other side was lifted with a potholder.

8. Cords are purposely fairly short on electric slow cookers. That's so they won't dangle and trip you. If possible, locate your cooker close to an outlet. If not, use an extension cord with an electrical rating at least as high as that of the cooker itself. Don't use the extension cord for other appliances while the crock is cooking. If you feel that the cord is heating up, unplug it and make some other arrangement, such as relocating the cooker closer to an outlet.

9. To protect the appearance of teflon-lined metal pots, use utensils with smooth edges to prevent scratching. Don't use steel wool, metal pads, or abrasive scouring powders to clean them. Instead, use a plastic sponge or nylon scouring pad and a thin paste of chlorinated cleanser and water. Scrub gently, then follow up with sudsy water; rinse and dry.

COOKING WITH THE CROCK

Cooking becomes second nature. Once we become accustomed to certain ways, it's not easy to change them. But the advantages of crockery cooking have, for many cooks, proven great enough to make the change worthwhile.

Keep these things in mind as you "re-program" yourself for success with slow cooking.

SELECTING RECIPES

Get acquainted with the types of dishes that the slow cooker does best: soups, stews and other long-cooking meat-and-vegetable combinations, vegetable combos, and fruit medleys. Anything that benefits from steam heat and extended cooking time works beautifully.

This may mean you can now fix recipes you've been avoiding because of long cooking times. It could add a whole new dimension to your meals.

The moist heat also makes ideal conditions to steam puddings. Most cookers can be used for dry baking, too. Some have special baker inserts that you can buy where slow cookers are sold. Or you can use one- or two-pound coffee cans with several layers of paper toweling over the top to absorb moisture. Cakes and quick breads come out deliciously moist, without ever turning on the oven. Come summer, that's a plus you'll appreciate.

Some cooks like to alternate recipes made in the crock, so everything doesn't come out looking like stew. Instead, try cooking a pot roast one day. The next meal from the cooker could be a whole chicken simmered with vegetables. Then, perhaps, fish chowder before you return to those old standbys—the stew variations.

Check the yield of a recipe against the capacity of your cooker. The crock should be at least half full. You can cover less food with foil. If the recipe makes too much for your cooker, cut the recipe.

Check the timing on the recipe to make sure it fits your time schedule for the day. Some people coordinate starting and stopping times with the times they will leave the house and return. Others who feel uncomfortable about leaving the house with an appliance on prefer to dovetail crock cooking with some other all-day project in the house.

CONVERTING RECIPES

After you get the hang of crock cooking, you will probably want to adapt some of your own favorite recipes to use in it. Here are things to keep in mind as you make the conversion.

Fresh milk products do not hold up well in lengthy crock cooking. If the dish needs a creamy look, use evaporated milk or substitute condensed cream soup right from the can. Or wait until the end of the cooking time to add milk, cream, or sour cream.

Pasta and instant rice get mushy when cooked six or eight hours. It's better to cook them separately and stir into the other ingredients near the end of the crock cooking time.

Some seasonings are unpredictable in the pot. Food seems less salty when the salt goes in at the beginning. If you'd like a saltier flavor, put half the salt in at the beginning, and add the rest at the end of the cooking time.

Long cooking develops stronger flavor in many herbs and spices. Try cutting the amount in standard recipes by half. You can always taste and add more later, but it's well-nigh impossible to subtract from flavor once it's there.

Some cooks prefer whole herbs and spices to crushed and ground forms. A whole bay leaf, for example, can be lifted out midway during the cooking time if the flavor is fully developed. It's also possible to tie whole spices in cheesecloth and remove them whenever you like. Through such experimentation, you'll be able to adjust seasonings to your own preference.

Because moisture is captured in the closed cooker, there isn't the evaporation that you expect in other forms of cooking. When converting recipes, try cutting the liquid in half. As with seasonings, more liquid can always be added later if needed.

Cooking time can be cut dramatically by heating the liquid called for in your recipe. Boiling water for soup, then measuring in a heat-proof cup, can reduce cooking length in a recipe that would otherwise take 12 or more hours.

TECHNIQUES WITH THE CROCK

Now for those things that Mother never told you about crock cooking (because there were no electric slow cookers in her day):

BEFORE THE LID GOES ON

1. Browning. For recipes such as stews and pot roast, it helps to brown meat in a skillet, then add to the pot. Some recipes tell you this isn't necessary, but our testing showed that a thorough browning of ten minutes or so produced more attractive and more tender meat.

But if you're looking for shortcuts and don't object to the pale appearance, it's possible to put everything in the pot at once. It does save a little time and cleanup.

2. Vegetables. Crock cooking gives different results with vegetables than standard cooking. In some types of crocks, vegetables take longer than the meat to reach tenderness. Experiment with your cooker; layering vegetables at the bottom of the pot may facilitate cooking.

3. Thickening. Recipes can be thickened at the beginning by stirring in three or four tablespoons of tapioca. Other ways are suggested in the next section on "After the Lid Comes Off."

4. Setting the control. Some recipes offer a choice of Low or High settings; others may indicate only one. But timing for High settings can be converted to Low by doubling the time length. And Low settings can convert to High by doing the reverse: cut time in half. Your choice will depend on the time available to you.

Low gives the tenderness and pleasant mingling of flavors for which crock cooking is famous. Cooking on High is more like standard cooking, but offers a handy shortcut when one is needed. It is advisable to stir occasionally when cooking on High.

DURING COOKING

The directions for cooking at the Low setting could be the easiest ever given: Do nothing. Peeking only lets out steam, and that means adding 15 to 20 minutes to the cooking time for it to build up again.

On the High setting, as mentioned, an occasional stir may be needed to prevent certain foods from sticking. And some recipes call for the addition of ingredients before the end of the cooking time. These are ingredients such as fish, mushrooms, or pasta, which cook in less time than the other recipe components.

AFTER THE LID COMES OFF

Most crock recipes give a range of cooking time such as "6 to 8 hours." Check at the end of the minimum time to see if the food is done to your liking. If it isn't tender, give it more time. If you're running late, turn a cooker that has been on Low up to High. That will cut remaining time in half.

On the other hand, if the meat is done in six hours and you'd planned dinner for a later hour, turn the cooker off and let the dish "rest" until serving time, rather than let the food overcook.

After cooking is the time to add those foods that cannot go in at the beginning: sour cream, cooked pasta, and the like. Stir them in just to heat through before serving.

If the sauce needs more thickening, take your choice of these methods:

1. Mix one tablespoon of flour or cornstarch for each cup of cooking liquid with enough cold water to make a smooth paste. Stir into the pot liquid and turn the heat up to high. With the lid off, stir the sauce until it reaches the thickness you like.

2. Taking a leaf from the French chef, mix equal parts of butter or margarine and flour. One tablespoon of this mixture will thicken a cup of pot liquid.

RECIPE CONVERSION TIME CHART

If original recipe calls for:	cook on Low for:	cook on High for:
1/4 to 1/2 hour	4 to 8 hours	1 1/2 to 2 1/2 hours
1/2 to 1 hour	6 to 8 hours	3 to 4 hours
1 to 3 hours	8 to 16 hours	4 to 6 hours